Schools
AROUND
the WORLD

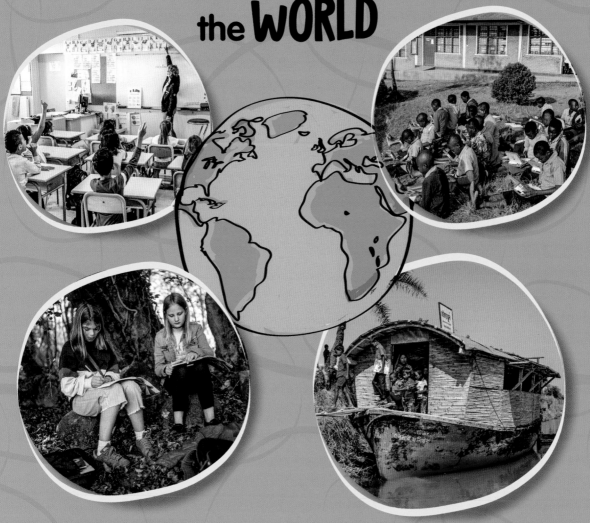

by Brenna Maloney

Children's Press®
An imprint of Scholastic Inc.

Library of Congress Cataloging-in-Publication Data
Names: Maloney, Brenna, author.
Title: Schools around the world/Brenna Maloney.
Description: First edition. | New York: Children's Press, an imprint of Scholastic Inc., 2021. |
    Series: Around the world | Includes index. | Audience: Ages 5–7. | Audience: Grades K–1. |
    Summary: "This book shows the many ways people learn around the world"— Provided
    by publisher.
Identifiers: LCCN 2021000136 (print) | LCCN 2021000137 (ebook) | ISBN 9781338768565 (library binding) |
    ISBN 9781338768572 (paperback) | ISBN 9781338768589 (ebook)
Subjects: LCSH: Schools—Cross–cultural studies—Juvenile literature. | Schools—Juvenile literature. |
    Education—Cross–cultural studies—Juvenile literature. | Education—Juvenile literature.
Classification: LCC LB1556 .M35 2021 (print) | LCC LB1556 (ebook) | DDC 371—dc23
LC record available at https://lccn.loc.gov/2021000136
LC ebook record available at https://lccn.loc.gov/2021000137

10 9 8 7 6 5 4 3 2 1   22 23 24 25 26

Printed in Heshan, China 62
First edition, 2022

Series produced by Spooky Cheetah Press
Cover and book design by Kimberly Shake

Photos ©: cover top left, 1 top left: Xavier Leoty/AFP/Getty Images; cover bottom left, 1 bottom left: Maja Hitij/Getty Images;
cover bottom right, 1 bottom right: Jonas Gratzer/LightRocket/Getty Images; cover top right, 1 top right: Joerg Boethling/
Alamy Images; 3: Hans Neleman/Getty Images; 4 left: imageBROKER/Alamy Images; 4 center: Bartosz Hadyniak/Getty
Images; 4 right: Ragnar Th. Sigurdsson/age fotostock; 5 left: Joe Sohm/Dreamstime; 5 right: Christian Ender/Getty Images;
6: Charly Triballeau/AFP/Getty Images; 7: SDI Productions/Getty Images; 8: Hap/Quirky China News/Shutterstock;
9: Mohamed Al Hwaity/Reuters/Alamy Images; 10: Erik De Castro/Reuters/Alamy Images; 11: Nguyen Vinh/Alamy Images;
12: Diego Barbieri/Kikapress; 14: Allison Joyce/Getty Images; 15: Rocco Rorandelli/TerraProject/co/Redux; 16: Vince937/
Dreamstime; 17: Brendan Esposito/Sydney Morning Herald/Fairfax Media/Getty Images; 18: robertharding/Alamy
Images; 19: Horizons WWP/Alamy Images; 20: Blaine Harrington/age fotostock; 21: Morsa Images/Getty Images; 22: Kirill
Kudryavtsev/AFP/Getty Images; 23: Vince Talotta/Toronto Star/Getty Images; 24: Sahlan Hayes/The Sydney Morning Herald/
Fairfax Media/Getty Images; 25: Yegor Aleyev/TASS/Getty Images; 26-27 background: Jim McMahon/Mapman®; 26 left:
Schultze/Zeitenspiegel/VISUM/Redux; 26 right: Layne Kennedy/Getty Images; 27 top: Imaginechina/AP Images; 27 center:
Sijori Images/Barcroft India/Getty Images; 27 bottom: Courtesy of Equal Education Law Centre; 28 left: Eitan Abramovich/
AFP/Getty Images; 28 center: Hug It Forward/Flickr; 28 right: Adriano Biondo; 29 top: Arne Hodalic/Corbis/Getty Images;
29 bottom left: Laurene Becquart/AFP/Getty Images; 29 bottom center: Adam Mork/Arcaid Images/Alamy Images;
29 bottom right: Bryan & Cherry Alexander Photography/Arctic Photo.

All other photos © Shutterstock.

TABLE of CONTENTS

JUST LIKE ME

Kids in every country around the world have a lot in common. They go to school and play. They have families and friends. Still, some things—like how and where they go to school—can be very different!

CHILE

KENYA

ICELAND

There are more than 480,000 school buses on the road in the United States.

UNITED STATES

INDIA

chapter 1
GETTING TO SCHOOL

To *go* to school, first you have to *get* to school. Lots of kids in the United States ride a yellow school bus. In the Netherlands, some kids take the S'Cool Bus. It's like a giant bike! But taking a bus is just one way to get to school.

Everyone on the S'Cool Bus helps the driver pedal.

In the United States, about 26 million kids ride a school bus each day.

Banpo students have to walk single file on this cliff path.

A lot of kids walk to school. But very few have a trip like students at Banpo Elementary School in China. Banpo students follow a narrow path in the side of a cliff. The path winds up, down, and around a mountain. It even goes through tunnels made of rock. Some students in Saudi Arabia don't walk to school. They climb! Every day, the kids climb concrete steps up the Fifa Mountains.

The stairs on the Fifa Mountains are very steep!

In one village in Vietnam, kids walk or swim through a river to get to school. Some villagers in the Philippines also have to travel on a river. But it is very deep. They can't walk. Some kids float to school on tire tubes. Others sail down the river on **bamboo** rafts.

Bamboo stems are hollow inside. That helps these rafts float.

These kids in Vietnam are getting a lift to school!

chapter 2
WHAT IS YOUR SCHOOL LIKE?

A school can be a building with many classrooms. Some schools are large. One school in India has more than 55,000 students. Others are small. A school in Italy had only one student and one teacher. But a school is not always a building.

Would you like to be the only student in your class?

These Indian students have gathered for a meeting before school.

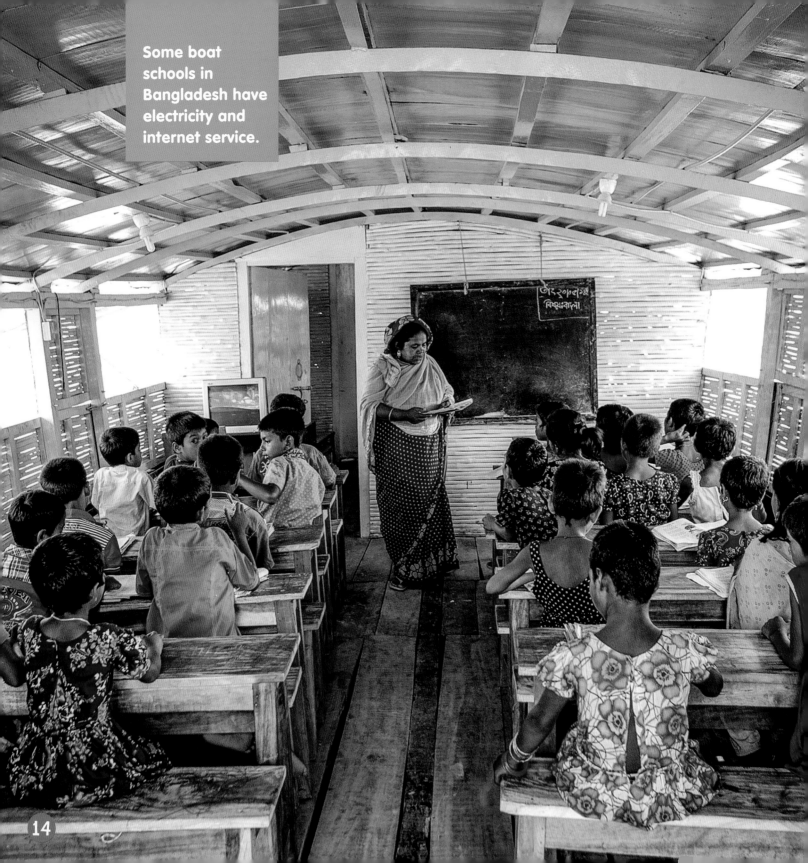

Some boat schools in Bangladesh have electricity and internet service.

In Bangladesh, where **flooding** is a problem, the school "building" might be a boat. That way, rising waters don't cut kids off from learning. Schooling and supplies in these boat schools are free to all students. In Finland, some classrooms are outside. These are called forest schools. The students play and explore. They learn about nature.

These students at a forest school in Finland are using rocks to solve a math problem!

Some kids in Australia live in the **outback**, far away from big cities. There are no schools nearby, so the kids have their lessons at home. These students work with their teachers over a two-way radio or the internet.

The outback is a big area in the center of Australia.

This Australian student is using a two-way radio that works like a walkie-talkie.

17

Kids in South Korea have one of the longest school years: 220 days.

chapter 3
TIME AT SCHOOL

In many places, kids start school when they are five. In Finland, kids start school when they are six. How much time kids spend in school can be different, too. France has the shortest school year among major nations. It is 144 days long. In many places in the United States, the school year is 180 days.

In the Netherlands, kids can start school on their fourth birthday. There is always someone new in class!

Not all kids have the weekends off, either. In Kenya, kids go to school six days a week. In Japan, school can be five days a week plus two Saturdays each month. The length of the school day varies, too. Mexico has one of the shortest days, and Taiwan has one of the longest.

In Mexico, the school day goes from 7:00 a.m. until noon.

In Taiwan, many students are in classes from 9:30 a.m. until 5:00 p.m.

chapter 4
WHAT DO YOU LEARN?

Kids learn to read and write in just about every school. They also study math and science. At some schools, kids learn in more than one language. Other schools have classes that are important to that country's **culture**. For example, in Armenia, kids learn **folk dancing**.

Armenia has more than 1,500 folk dances.

In parts of Canada, most lessons are taught in French and English.

23

These Australian students are learning surfing skills and water safety.

A lot of schools offer fun classes. Many schools in Russia teach **beekeeping**. Kids learn to handle bees and collect honey. In Iceland, all kids are taught how to knit. And in Australia, students who live by the ocean learn how to surf.

A school may be a building, a boat, or even a forest. But they all give children a chance to learn. How do these schools around the world compare to yours?

Kids who learn about beekeeping need to wear protective clothing.

IF YOU LIVED HERE . . .

Getting there is half the fun! Let's look at some interesting ways kids get to school.

UNITED STATES
Students living on Mackinac Island in Michigan take snowmobiles to school in winter.

COLOMBIA
Some kids have to cross the Rio Negro to get to school. They zoom down a zip line at a speed of 50 miles (80 kilometers) per hour.

CHINA
Until recently, kids who went to school in Atule'er village in Sichuan Province had to climb a hill on a steel ladder that is 2,625 feet (800 meters) high.

INDONESIA
Some kids in Sumatra walk on a tightrope 30 feet (9 meters) above a flowing river. Then they hike another 7 miles (11 kilometers) through a forest to get to school.

SOUTH AFRICA
In Nqutu, KwaZulu-Natal, the daily walk to school can be 10 miles (16 kilometers) long.

A CLOSER LOOK

Can you imagine going to school in any of these places?

Argentina

River Plate Institute is a school in Buenos Aires. It is located in the River Plate Stadium, which is also home to a professional soccer team.

Guatemala

This school is made from **recycled** plastic bottles stuffed with plastic trash and covered with cement. The community worked together on the building.

Germany

Kindergartners in Karlsruhe go to a school that looks like a giant cat. The cat's mouth is the door. Classrooms are in the cat's belly.

Nenets kids who don't go to school have to study on their own.

India

Some families in India can't afford to send their children to school. Instead, they can go to the "Free School Under the Bridge" in Delhi.

Denmark

The Ørestad Gymnasium school in Copenhagen has no classrooms. Instead, students relax and study in spots called "drums."

Russia

The Nenets people are **nomadic** reindeer herders who live in Siberia, far from any cities. Many children go to **boarding school** from spring through fall.

GLOSSARY

bamboo (bam-BOO) a tropical plant with a hollow, woody stem

beekeeping (BEE-kee-ping) raising honeybees

boarding school (BOR-ding SKOOL) a school that students may live in during the school year

culture (KUHL-chur) the ideas, customs, traditions, and way of life of a group of people

flooding (FLUH-ding) the overflowing of a body of water beyond its banks

folk dancing (FOHLK DAN-sing) a kind of dance that is native to a particular area or group

nomadic (noh-MAD-ik) traveling from place to place instead of living in the same place all the time

outback (OUT-bak) places in Australia that are far from cities

recycled (ree-SYE-kuhld) processed and made ready for reuse (materials such as glass, plastic, newspapers, and aluminum cans)

INDEX

ABOUT THE AUTHOR

Brenna Maloney is a writer and an editor. Maloney attended Riley Elementary School in New Castle, Indiana. Today she lives and works in Washington, D.C., with her family.